"Powerfully written with stra… Anderson takes any and all dark clouds and turns… blessings you learn from, grow from, and use as fuel to make life better than you ever thought possible."

Matt Furey, author of *The Unbeatable Man*

"As you turn these pages, you and Jim will explore the difficulties of the human drama. You'll be encouraged to ask soul-searching questions that staircase up to the only question you'll ever really need to ask yourself – the **Secret Seven-Word Question**. Answer this one and poof! You're free!"

Peter Ragnar, Author of *How Long Do You Choose To Live* and *The Awesome Science of Luck*

"As a longtime fan of Jim's approach to life, I was thrilled to read his beautiful philosophy in *How to Find a Silver Lining in Every Dark Cloud*. If you've been seeking a practical way to find good things in your life no matter what, this is your answer. It's like having an uplifting, motivating conversation with a good friend… in fact, that's exactly what it is."

Veronica Hughes, Professional Editor and Author of *The Pinball Path to God: A Spiritual Autobiography*

"Do you want inspired living? Do you want an astonishing, fun new way to create peace and happiness in your life? Read *How To Find A Silver Lining In Every Dark Cloud* by Jim M Anderson. It changed my life and will change yours too! Jim's book is The Key: The Missing Secret To The Life You Want Now!"

Ken Hazlin, www.EyeExerciseSecrets.com

"I truly appreciate the clarity and insight you share in the book and every day in your life. Your wisdom and open heart, combined with your joyful outlook, present a force for good that I find truly amazing."

Lisa Ariel Morrison, Corpus Christi, TX

"What can I say about Jim Anderson? This divine gift-giver of awareness has assisted me in so many ways. I could probably write a book myself about things I am doing differently. I am meditating. I search for my center in daily activities and physical endeavors. I clean bathrooms. I have compassion for the ping-pong champion who trashed my ski condo. I ask myself the secret seven-word question multiple times per week. Acquaintances approach me for advice – I can only assume because of the energy emanating from my core. I have regained a child's mind. I sleep well over the weekend when my job is at risk. I'm planning my dreams…and fulfilling them. These are just a few experiences for which I am grateful to Jim."

Brad Ludford, CFO, Exempla St. Joseph Hospital

"As Jim moves through his personal challenges, he'll keep you on the edge of your seat. The sheer simplicity of his concluding message may make you laugh and cry as you come to realize the immense value of adversity."

Tony Balistreri, Executive Vice President, Roaring Lion Publishing

"*How to Find a Silver Lining in Every Dark Cloud* may on the surface appear to be a Pollyanna view that everything always happens for a good reason. The typical view of a silver lining that someone else is controlling our destiny, but this book is about just the opposite. We are responsible for everything that happens in our lives. We are not victims. We cannot blame God, our parents, or even our ethnic background. The seven-word question, when taken seriously, is life-changing because it leads us to greater self-awareness and personal accountability.

This book will introduce you to the concept of locus of control, clarity cycle, the power of attraction, and positive affirmation… but it is only the beginning of a journey to self-awareness, a journey to personal freedom, and in the end, a journey to success in business and happiness as an individual. I know. I have been on this journey with Jim Anderson for several years, and I know that playful, persistent, patient practice in applying the seven-word question has significantly changed my life for the better."

Pat Finneran, CEO, Sabreliner Corporation

"There are special people who come into your life at the right time to assist you with challenges you face, and Jim has been that person since day one. I have known Jim and have been applying the principles taught in *How to Find a Silver Lining in Every Dark Cloud* since 1998. I can say without a shadow of a doubt that this book will impact your life in a major way if you open up to Jim's unique discoveries recorded in it.

In *How to Find a Silver Lining in Every Dark Cloud*, Jim delivers honest, heart-wrenching, life-changing, and pivotal life experiences – one right after the other – that have molded him into the amazing person he is today. I have heard these stories at least a dozen times, and the power of each message never loses its zeal or its profound impact. There is no one else who welcomes a problem into his life with as much grace and ease as Jim does. He treats every challenge as a blessing in disguise. Jim's mission is to touch the lives of a million people, and he lives this every day.
I'm a witness to his approach and this book will touch a million people *plus* and change the landscape of self-development.

I've been applying Jim's **Secret Seven-Word Question** for over 11 years, and each time I grow mentally, physically, emotionally and spiritually. The best part about this question is its simplicity. It's the most profound seven words when faced with a challenge or the feeling that someone has wronged you. By applying the principles taught in this book, I have less stress, more peace of mind, my hair doesn't turn gray over small stuff, I experience life's subtleties with more fervor, I accept every problem as a lesson to learn from, and have permanently shredded my 'victim card.' Each time I read this book, I receive a new nugget of wisdom to apply in my life to achieve higher levels of awareness and satisfaction.

Grab this book! It reveals the *only* true secret to a fulfilling, happy life. You will be amazed at how on target this last statement is."

> **Vince Palko, Author of *Tackling Life's Problems* and Two-Time Hall of Fame Linebacker**

"The ability to connect the significant challenges in our lives with our most fundamental strength: that is what Jim Anderson has discovered. In a world where we are asked to react to more and more complex events at an ever-quickening pace, the tendency is for us to seek help from afar. Jim introduces a method – no, a way of living – that places all of this within one's control. The simplicity of the concept is the attractant; the degree of difficulty is up to each one of us."

> **Sheldon Stadnyk MD, CMO**
> **North Colorado Medical Center, Greeley, CO**

How To Find a Silver Lining In Every Dark Cloud

Jim M Anderson

How To Find a Silver Lining In Every Dark Cloud
by Jim M Anderson

Copyright © 2009 by FitToLead.com

All Rights Reserved

Cover design by Vincent Palko – www.AdToons.com

No part of this publication may be reproduced or transmitted in any form or by any means, electronic, mechanical, photocopying, recording, scanning, or otherwise, without the written permission of the copyright owner, except as permitted under Section 107 or 108 of the United States Copyright Act. Requests for permission or further information should be addressed to jim@fittolead.com.

This publication is designed to provide accurate and authoritative information in regard to the subject matter covered. It is sold with the understanding that the author and the publisher are not engaged in rendering legal, accounting, therapeutic, or other professional services. The advice of a competent professional person should be sought if there are further questions.

Visit our website: **www.fittolead.com** to sign up for FREE success tips delivered to your email inbox every day.

Disclaimer

The content presented in this book is not intended to be prescriptive in any way. It simply reflects a collection of experiences, ideas, and practices that have significantly improved the life and well-being of its author and his family. The information included herein should not interfere with any advice you are receiving under the direction or care of any other professional. The creators, producers, participants, advertisers, and distributors of this book disclaim any liabilities or loss as a result of the ideas or suggestions contained herein.

Dedicated to my wife and best friend Kristan who has loved, challenged, and encouraged me to delight in "what is" without exception.

Table of Contents

INTRODUCTION	1 - 7
PART ONE: Sleepwalking Through Life	8 - 15
Nightmare on Burroughs Street	9
Distressing But Necessary Wake-up Call	10
A Long, Lonely Night – What's the Heck is Happening to Me?	11
Mad As Hell – Purging my Pent-Up Anger	12
PART TWO: Waking From My Deluded Slumber	16 - 26
Truth Begins to Dawn: Facing the Cold, Hard Facts	17
Taking an Honest Look at Myself in the Mirror	21
Acceptance, Forgiveness, and Appreciation - Essential First Steps	22
Moment of Truth – Would I Stay or Would I Go?	25
PART THREE: Questioning Everything	27 - 37
Reclaiming Creative Responsibility for my Life, Marriage and Family	28
Awakening the Transformative Power of Questions	31
Fortifying my Observer Self & Refining the Quality of my Questions	35
PART FOUR: Divulging the Hidden Power of Introspective Questions	38 - 44
Practicality First, Profundity Later	39
What if What I Focus On Grows? Then What?	40
Practice Makes Perfect-Applying Productivity Questions	43

PART FIVE: Unveiling the Secret Seven-Word Wonder	45 - 56
Deeper Questions + Reflections = Unfathomable Meaning & Purpose	46
The Secret Seven-Word Question That's Transforming my Life	48
Protest If You Must, But Don't Make the Mistake of Walking Away	49
Don't Believe A Word I Say – Only Trust Your Own Direct Experience	52
This Seven-Word Wonder is a World Champion Question	52
PART SIX: Success Stories	57 - 72
This Question Is Designed to Be a Living Meditation	58
Show Me Some Proof	59
Mining More Silver Linings in my Life's Dark Clouds	61
Awed by the Courage of my Coaching Clients	63
A Few Success Stories I've Been Privileged to Witness	64
PART SEVEN: Will the Seven-Word Secret Work for Me?	73 - 78
Putting this Secret Seven-Word Question to Work for You	74
Seven Simple but Profound Tips for putting the Secret Seven-Word Question to the Test	75
Appreciative Epilogue	79 - 85
Contact Us	86
About the Author	87

Introduction

You're About To Discover
a Radical Seven-Word Question
That Will Show You How To Find
a Silver Lining in Every Dark Cloud
That You Think Is Holding You Back.

Dear Friend,

Hi! My name is Jim Anderson and I'm a highly successful and fulfilled human being, and you can become one too. I live the life of my dreams with my wife in a beautiful home in the mountains, and I have five wonderful children who have grown up to become successes themselves.

But it wasn't always this way. My road to success has been littered with many, many gut-wrenching challenges and setbacks.

Although I haven't had the chance to meet you personally yet, I know that we share a lot in common. You wouldn't be reading this if you weren't wrestling with some significant challenges, searching for a way to live a more effective, more productive, more meaningful and balanced life. Well, you are not alone, my friend. You see, there was a time when I was:

- Depressed and emotionally unstable.
- Consumed by workaholism.
- Mentally spent and physically exhausted.
- Out of touch with reality and spinning out of control.
- Burdened with debt and living beyond my means.
- Overwhelmed with family responsibilities.
- Significantly overweight and out of shape.
- Feeling trapped and miserable in my job.
- Fighting for my life in the face of kidney disease.
- Lacking self-confidence.
- Unhappy and constantly whining and complaining to myself.
- Consumed in self-hatred and living a life of quiet desperation.
- Spiritually dead.

I thought there was no hope – in fact, there were many times when I gave up hope completely. However, I was able to turn everything around. **And it all began with this Secret Seven-Word Question I started asking myself.**

You might be thinking that there's no way a seven-word question could <u>possibly</u> do <u>all</u> this. I thought the same thing. So I started disclosing this secret question in my coaching sessions with Fortune 500 executives, as well as young men and women in their 20s who were just getting their feet on the ground...and everyone in between.

The results were astonishing. <u>After</u> they cursed me for posing such a question, I witnessed careers transformed, obstacles overcome, marriages saved, and entire lives turned around.

Again, all because of this one, unusual seven-word question.

This dramatic Secret Seven-Word Question…

- **LEAPFROGS you clear over your limiting beliefs,** no matter how paralyzing they are…no matter how long they've been weighing you down…<u>**and even if you don't know they exist.**</u>

- Reveals the **TRUE** cause of all the **FEAR** in your life…as well as **how to eliminate fear <u>on demand</u>.**

- Will help you **rise above ANY mental or emotional stress or pain.**

- Puts **YOU** in control of your career and **guides you on the path to creating financial freedom.**

- Gives you the **COURAGE to face and overcome physical illness.**

- **Heals dysfunctional relationships** with your spouse, family members, friends, and co-workers.

- **Reveals the TRUE cause of all the FRUSTRATIONS** in your life…as well as how to remove them for good.

- Opens the door to **finding MEANING and purpose in**

life even if you've "achieved it all," yet still feel empty inside.

And YES…<u>all</u> of this is possible with just one unusual seven-word question – which has <u>never</u> been revealed in any self-development book, course, or coaching program until <u>now</u>. For the first time in print, I am revealing this **Secret Seven-Word Question** to the general public. But before I do, I want to share the story of my own uphill struggle, reveal how I discovered this amazing this question, and show you how it has radically improved my life. Then I will unveil this **Secret Seven-Word Question** so you can immediately begin to:

- Overpower limiting beliefs and give creative expression to your highest aspirations.

- Transform dysfunctional relationships into sustainable friendships.

- Conquer fear and liberate newfound courage.

- Convert emotional pain into building blocks of self-confidence.

- Move from being overwhelmed to balanced.

- Pay off debt and create financial freedom.

- Triumph over physical illness or injury and jumpstart a healthy and vibrant new you.

- Free yourself from feeling trapped in a job you dislike and take control of your career.

- Overpower that nagging pang of emptiness that hides in the pit of your stomach and start living a life filled with meaning and purpose.

You are only seven simple words from building a better life! So let me tell you the story of how I discovered this question and some of the many ways it has blessed me.

Sincerely,

Jim M Anderson

Jim M Anderson
Samurai of Self-Development

Part One
Sleepwalking Through Life

Nightmare on Burroughs Street

In 1992, I was living in a nice home in the Midwest, married to my best friend, and raising five amazing children. I worked a responsible job that provided economic security for my family. I had done all I had been trained to do and, by most people's standards, I was leading and living a very successful life. I was performing well in my job, and I held up a positive appearance on the outside. But inside, a deep, dark, depressed angst was gradually overtaking me.

I was dying a slow death. I was talking the talk but not walking the walk. I frequently pontificated to others that my priorities were God, family, and career, in that order.

Let's examine the truth of the matter. In reality, I was living a lie. I spent no time or energy cultivating my relationship with God. Although I had been blessed with a remarkable wife and five beautiful children, I was letting them down and wasn't even aware of it. During the workweek, I was asked to make just one family commitment – be home from work in time for dinner at 6:15. I was leaving at 4 am and generally never made it home before 7 or 8 at night. Worse yet, I never called to tell my wife when I wouldn't be home for dinner. Imagine what it was like for her to be bringing up five children under the age of seven and continuously being let down by the person who had committed to be there to help her raise this family.

Distressing But Necessary Wake-up Call

One Friday evening, I again arrived home late. I opened the door and, before I could set one foot inside, my wife greeted me with a suitcase with two days' clothes. She looked me in the eye and delivered one of the most painful, shocking, and yet loving gifts she could have given me at that time. She handed me the bag and simply said, "Jim, here is a suitcase already packed – YOU HAVE TWO DAYS TO FIGURE OUT IF YOU WANT TO BE IN THIS FAMILY ANY MORE."

I stood there in shock as my world of fraudulent, fake appearances imploded and came tumbling down around me. I reached out, took the bag, and stumbled toward my car in a state of shock.

"I spent the longest, loneliest, most challenging weekend of my life."

I checked into a motel and spent the longest, loneliest, and most challenging weekend of my life. I had two days to discern what was happening to me and make perhaps the most significant decision of my life to that point. Would I stay or would I go?

A Long, Lonely Night – What the Heck Is Happening to Me?

For the first twenty-four hours, I was mostly in shock and denial. I kept trying to justify my workaholism, and I whined about how unfair my wife was being. Couldn't she see how hard I was working? If only she could realize how much I was sacrificing for our family! Why couldn't she understand how difficult it was to be <u>me</u>? Couldn't she just appreciate all that I was doing and stop complaining about what I <u>wasn't</u> doing? If only she would change, then everything would be fine!

What the heck is happening to me!? Although this was a seven-word question that commanded my full attention at the time, it is <u>not</u> the **Secret Seven-Word Question**. But had I known the secret question at that time, I would have dealt with this challenging situation much more gracefully and effectively than I did.

"Is someone coming to save <u>me</u>?"

This train of thought did nothing but increase the pain and deepen the trap of ignorant obliviousness and denial that I had been living in. These were "victim questions" and they represented a feeble attempt to once again try to make someone else accountable for the mess I had created. All that these pitiful questions did was make the longest, darkest, night of my life even longer, darker, and harder.

Mad As Hell – Purging My Pent-Up Anger

When it became evident that my usual victim approach was not going to bail me out, I got mad as hell. I began cursing God. I said:

- Damn you! How dare you allow this to happen to me!
- If you were a loving God, you wouldn't allow me to go through this!
- Where the hell are you when I need you, God!?
- How can an omnipresent God abandon me like this!?
- God, why are you punishing me?
- Is someone out there coming to save me?
- Hey God, why don't you wave your almighty wand and fix this mess!?
- What kind of God would stand by and watch me fail like this?

Then I cursed the pope. I told him, "I go to your church every week. I enrolled my kids in your schools. I give a steady stream of my income to your causes. I obey the leaders of your church. I volunteer my time to serve the parish. And look what all that brought me! Nothing but insurmountable problems! My marriage is in disarray, and it's entirely your fault!

Then I cursed my parents. I found myself thinking how my mom always used to say, "There's a silver lining in every dark storm cloud." At that moment, I protested and screamed, "That's a heap of crap!" This was the darkest storm I'd faced at that point in my life. It was so dark and scary that there couldn't possibly be any silver <u>anywhere</u> in the storm that raged around me.

Then there was my dad. He was famous for passing on a lesson that my grandpa had taught him – "It's important to turn all the minuses you encounter in life into plusses." Screw that! I hate math, and besides, this minus I'm being leveled by has no potential to become a plus. I was in the midst of a Class 5 Emotional Hurricane here, and I sure as heck wasn't seeing any opportunities to turn minuses into plusses!

Then, I went after my best teachers and my favorite coaches. Next, it was time to blame my friends, to revile my relatives, and to berate every mere acquaintance I could recall.

Finally, I turned inward and began to slay <u>myself</u> with my own brand of negative, degrading self-talk. I shouted what seemed at the time to be real pearls of truth and wisdom. Some of the best ones included:

- This is bull #*#@!
- Life sucks! No, <u>I</u> suck!
- I'm getting screwed here!
- Those idiots lied to me!
- This isn't happening to me! (Talk about blatant denial!)
- Successful people are lucky and I'm not!
- I'm a failure!
- I'm sick of being rejected!
- No one loves me!
- I can't go on another day like this!
- I'm such a loser!
- Something's got to change here!

Alone in the darkness of my hotel, I continued cursing everything and everyone who came to mind. And OOOHHHH did it ever feel great! My rage flowed unobstructed for a few hours.

I had never experienced rage like this before. On one hand, giving voice to it was liberating. On the other hand, it scared the daylights out of me and triggered a major round of guilt. I finally reached a complete state of exhaustion and fell fast asleep for about an hour and a half.

Part Two

Waking from My Deluded Slumber

Truth Begins to Dawn: Facing the Cold, Hard Facts

I was jolted awake as the first rays of dawn streamed through the window of my motel room. As my eyes adapted to the brightness and my nose adjusted to the musty smell of the dreary drapes, I felt a strong feeling of dread consuming me. I felt the weight of the huge choice I faced bearing down on my chest to the point where I became short of breath. I rolled off the edge of my bed and landed in a kneeling position, where I began to pray and plead with anyone or anything that would listen.

I came to the realization that my life wasn't working. I had reached a breaking point. I had finally come to a place where I was ready to face the truth. I was now willing to surrender and do whatever would be required to acknowledge and gradually change the miserable circumstances that I found myself in.

"Changing my circumstances would require a transformative change in me."

As the full sun peeked over the horizon, it illuminated a challenging but liberating truth that was beginning to make itself known within my heart.

The tension in my chest began to ease as this heartfelt awareness surged forth into my consciousness. It was inescapably clear to me that I was the cause of the circumstances I now found myself in. No one else had done this to me. I was fully responsible for my situation, and no one else was going to save me from facing this reality.

I was gradually awakening to the fact that changing my circumstances would require a transformative change in me. I felt an indescribable exhilaration mounting. Some part of me was enthused about the reality of my situation and the challenge it posed. This was a new but compelling feeling. I wanted to trust it, but I lacked the confidence to commit myself completely.

Then, without warning, an opposing force reared its ugly head. It protested, suggesting that I was a victim, that I could not be held responsible, that I was doing the best I could. This was a much more familiar voice, one that was used to dominating my awareness without question or challenge. I both feared and secretly despised this voice. In that moment, it had the audacity to suggest that:

- *If only* my wife would change, then things would be better.

- *If only* my parents had raised me differently, then I would be happy.
- *If only* my teachers and coaches hadn't lied to me, then my life would be working better.
- *If only* my friends would be more understanding, then I'd have healthier relationships.
- *If only* God had not abandoned me, then my life would be on track.

How arrogant and out of touch I was! Once again, my train of thought was trying to pin the blame of my situation on those who loved me most. These were the very people who had sacrificed a great deal to lay a hell of a foundation for me to thrive upon.

Suddenly, my awareness shifted back to that part of me that was enthused about making a positive change. I stood up and committed to own my current situation and resolved to take a greater level of responsibility for my circumstances. Up to that time, I had fallen into the habit of handing over creative responsibility for my life to everyone but the person who could actually do something productive with it – ME! I had allowed myself to become a pitiful excuse for a human being. I had been sleepwalking through life, playing along in a game of make-believe, and building a false self-image that was now under attack on every front.

On the surface, things looked great, just like a termite-ridden home can look great at first glance. Upon closer examination, however, it became abundantly clear that I wasn't cutting it. I was living a full-fledged lie, and the truth was now slapping me silly.

In that moment, it dawned on me that my strategy of playing the game of false appearances, blame, and avoidance was no longer working. In fact, it was becoming quite evident that it had <u>never</u> worked. This habit pattern was the cause of this mess I found myself in.

In a flash of realization, I felt the hint of enthusiasm from a moment ago transform into a source of courage that rose up from a place deep within me, from a place that I had not known existed. A newly emerging part of me revealed itself as a peaceful, powerful presence that commanded me to face the truth by taking a long, sobering, self-examining look in the mirror. By facing this new aspect of myself, I was choosing to reclaim creative control of my life.

I had only 24 hours left before making the most important decision of my life and communicating it to my wife. I was not going to squander this time with another moment of whimpering.

Taking an Honest Look at Myself in the Mirror

It was time to get some fresh air. I decided to leave the motel and take a long hike in the woods at a Metropark, Oak Openings, just west of town. Upon arriving, I immediately left the more populated area of the park to seek greater seclusion. As I slipped deeper and deeper into the woods, I found myself drifting into a quality and depth of reflective self-honesty that was new to me.

"It would be essential for me to forgive myself before attempting to change my life."

I began to sincerely examine my life in great detail. The combination of the natural setting and my desire to uncover the facts and face the truth opened the door to a much more productive line of thought and reflection. I began to question and examine what I espoused as my priorities. I then honestly assessed how these priorities lined up with how I had been investing my time, energy, and money. The results of this exercise were devastating at first.

As I mentioned earlier, I was famous for pontificating that my priorities were God, family, and career, in that order. When I examined my life under a microscope, I quickly came to the conclusion that I had been living a lie. I could choose to be honest and admit that my true priorities were actually career, career, and career; change nothing; and lose my marriage, family, and who knows what else. Or I could work with my wife and kids to redefine my priorities and reorganize the ways in which I was investing my time, energy, and money to be more consistently aligned with what I believed.

As I sat beneath a huge oak tree pondering this, it became abundantly clear that I cared deeply for my wife and kids, and that I was willing to do whatever was required to get my marriage back on track and regain the trust and respect of my family.

Acceptance, Forgiveness, and Appreciation – Essential First Steps

Before I could begin to rebuild my marriage and reclaim my family, I would first have to acknowledge and accept the reality of the challenges I faced. This two-day forced sabbatical had served me well, enabling me to own the reality I found myself in.

Next, it became evident that it would be essential to forgive myself for my failures before attempting to change and rebuild my life. I spent the next few hours sitting by a stream with a notepad and pen, journaling away. As I engaged in this very constructive process, it became apparent that this was more than an "action item" that I would simply check off my to-do list later that day. I was birthing a forgiveness exercise that would evolve into an annual practice that would benefit me for many years to come.

While journaling at the river's edge, I took time to:
- Acknowledge my feelings of inadequacy.
- Identify my weaknesses.
- Recognize my shortcomings.
- Admit my shortfalls.
- Own up to my failed promises.

I was not used to this level of self-honesty. It had a tremendous cleansing effect. I began to feel literally lighter, happier, and more alive as I examined this baggage that I had been hauling around in my soul. It had been weighing me down for years, and the toll it had taken was huge. With each stroke of my pen, I off-loaded this garbage, one item at a time. Once I had laundered all of it out of my system, I created an impromptu forgiveness ritual and let it all go.

My exercise of self-absolution carved out an empty space that left me naturally encouraged to extend my forgiveness exercise to include my concept of God and all the people I had spent the previous day cursing and blaming for my circumstances. Once again, I let my pen do its magic. Soon, I felt a heavy burden of guilt lift off my chest and transform into a sustained buoyancy and lightness that I hadn't experienced in a long time. I could breathe again! I felt abundant life pumping through my veins.

Suddenly, tears of gratitude flowed down my cheeks as gracefully as the river flowed along its banks. My heart was overflowing with a deep sense of gratitude and appreciation. I was grateful that my wife loved me enough and had the courage to present me with a long-overdue wake-up call. I was also grateful that I found it in me to face the truth and accept this loving wake-up call as the gift it was intended to be. An expanded level of self-esteem and self-confidence began to radiate within me.

As I drove home, I watched the sun set. It was beautiful, and I knew that it signified the end of my two-day retreat. The onset of darkness also held the challenge and promise of a transformative change that lay before me.

Moment of Truth – Would I Stay or Would I Go?

I pulled into our driveway as dusk gave way to darkness. There was an eerie quiet in our neighborhood. Our kids were already asleep and most of the lights in the house were out.

Would I stay or would I go? Although I had pondered many questions over the past weekend, none was as important to me as this one. (Once again, this is not the **Secret Seven-Word Question** I have been promising. Be patient – it's coming, and I promise it will be worth the wait!)

I walked in and looked into my wife's eyes. Tears began to flow. I first apologized for my failure to deliver on the commitments I had made as a husband and father. I then thanked her for the courage it took to give me the priceless gift of my forced, unplanned sabbatical.

We sat down and had a long conversation. I disclosed many of my reflections and revelations from the weekend. She then told me what it had been like for her over these many months of being abandoned and left alone to raise our family.

After listening carefully, I said that I wanted to recommit to developing myself into the best person, husband, dad, friend, and businessman that I was capable of becoming. At the same time, I also openly acknowledged the reality of the centrifugal force that had been habitually pulling me off course for years. I told my wife that I honestly didn't know if I had it in me to make the changes that would be required to transform myself and become the husband and dad that she and my kids deserved. I was willing to give it my all if they would be willing to work with me.

> *"It was time to devote my full attention to clarifying my priorities and values."*

She accepted my recommitment pledge, articulated what she expected of me, and made it very clear that she intended to hold me fully accountable.

Part Three
Questioning Everything

Reclaiming Creative Responsibility for My Life, Marriage, and Family

My wife and I spent many late nights talking through the inner challenges we faced. We worked together to establish and agree on a set of priorities and values that we would realign our lives around.

As we considered the changes that we would have to make, it became evident that the individual challenges that I faced would require my commitment to some rigorous work for at least a year. It was time for me to devote my full attention to clarifying my priorities and values, examining how well my current job aligned with my purpose, assessing the type of work I wanted to do, and rebuilding trust with my family. I had to make some radical changes to regain balance in my life if we were to have any real chance of success.

After many hours of honest conversation and weighing every possible option, I decided that the only way to successfully get my life back on track was to resign from my job and focus on finding work that better aligned with my purpose. I wanted a job that would allow me more flexibility to meet the ever-increasing requirements of our family.

Over the next couple of months, we put a plan in place and then implemented the plan. I resigned, cashed out our retirement fund (with the early withdrawal penalty and tax hit), and started the rigorous work required to get my professional life and our family life back on a solid footing. This was by far the biggest risk we had ever taken.

One year later, we decided to forgo employment and start our own business. This presented a compelling challenge, but would allow much greater control over my schedule.

I was ill-prepared for what happened next. I had made the grave error of overestimating the value that I could offer in the marketplace. I also <u>way</u> underestimated the challenge that we were entering. In our first twelve months of business, we generated a whopping $6,000 in gross revenue and tallied up expenses of almost $90,000! It doesn't take a genius to figure out that it's impossible to raise five kids when the company providing the major source of income is performing like this.

I spent many long days frantically conceptualizing and creating an offering of consulting products and services. Then, I took my very best ideas to the market and faced one rejection after another. At first, the only people who would hire me were friends of my family who felt sorry for me.

I'd work all day and then spend most of every night:
- Worrying about our retirement savings that had evaporated.
- Fretting over bills that seemed insurmountable.
- Ashamed that I had squandered the modest fortune I'd inherited at birth.
- Tormented by the possibility that I'd fail and put my family through hell (again).
- Wondering if I really had it in me to succeed.

One cold winter night, I was tossing and turning in bed. I had slept restlessly for about two hours when I was jolted awake by a bout of cold sweats. Everything I thought I knew was proving itself to be pretty useless. My confidence had been deeply shaken, and the grips of depression and fear were attempting to tighten their grasp on my throat. Although I was in a household with six people who genuinely loved me, I felt completely alone.

As I lay there, my disturbed feelings fiercely tempted me to reclaim the same victim mentality that had dominated me during my two-day sabbatical a year earlier. Even though I knew this victim approach had produced miserable results, some demented aspect of me wanted to pick up right where I had left off. It wanted to once again revel in the joys of whining, blaming, and cursing God and everyone else for the challenging situation I now found myself in.

Fortunately, a wiser, more rational part of me reminded me that this brilliant approach hadn't worked worth a damn back then, and it sure as hell wouldn't work any better now. Thankfully, I listened and avoided repeating the follies of that dismal drama.

Awakening the Transformative Power of Questions

Once again, in the midst of this overwhelming state of confusion, a powerful, peaceful presence within me interrupted the stress and strain. Much to my surprise, this awareness hinted that the challenging times like the ones I was facing always carried within them hidden treasures. All I had to do was look for them.

A familiar irritation leapt forth from my subconscious and protested. Yeah, right! Just like the silver lining that's supposedly hiding in the dark storm clouds of life!

This sarcastic outburst transported me back to my childhood. At the age of six, I was unexpectedly sidelined by a severe heart condition that confined me to bed for six months, followed by another six months in a wheelchair. I remembered my mom consoling me as I struggled to make sense of a situation that seemed so unfair and unfortunate to my six-year old awareness. One afternoon, my mom sat at my bedside encouraging me through a bout of despair. She lovingly stroked my cheek, smiled, and said, "Jim, there is a silver lining in every dark storm cloud in life. All we have to do is look for it."

> *"This seedpod of wisdom did little to quiet the depression that lurked within me."*

At the time, this seedpod of wisdom did little to quiet the depression that lurked within me. I felt victimized by my heart condition, which I thought was robbing me of the playtime that I deserved. Now, I see that I had no idea what my mom was talking about. I am, however, very grateful to her. She had planted an idea that would play a crucial part in revealing the powerful, life-changing, **Secret Seven-Word Question** that would radically improve my life decades later.

This memory primed an invisible pump, as a powerful presence calmly reasserted control of my mental state. This presence suggested that I try asking myself reflective questions whenever I faced situations that presented doubt, difficulty, complaint, or confusion. It challenged me to just try it, to playfully and patiently persist in the practice of asking myself questions and then responding to them in a reflective manner. It promised that something profound would reveal itself through this discipline – but that many rounds of practice would be required.

"I gradually became aware of negative self-talk and beliefs that gave them life."

What the heck, I thought. What did I have to lose? I decided to give it a try and see what happened. The source of irritation that had protested loudly a bit earlier now tucked its tail between its legs and crept away dejected, confused, and defeated.

The initial questions were pretty weak, but they served an important purpose.

These are some of the questions that I posed most frequently at first:

- What in the hell was I thinking? Stupid ass! (Is that really a question?)
- Why do these bad things keep happening to poor ol' me?
- How ignorant can I be?
- Does my frequent tendency to fail mean that I'm a failure?
- Do I have it in me to be successful?

It's natural to begin with questions like this. At that time, I was new to the game of conscious introspection. I was temporarily incapable of posing and reflecting on the more powerful questions that would gradually reveal themselves through more practice. Playing the game with these weaker questions served an important purpose. It gradually made me aware of my habits of negative self-talk and the underlying subconscious beliefs that fed them. By posing and reflecting on these early questions, I began to scrub the victim mentality out of my system, one stroke at a time.

Fortifying My Observer Self and Refining the Quality of My Questions

Sometimes I'd lose patience with this process of posing questions. On occasion, mild fits of frustration would once again take control, demanding that I suspend the questioning process and return to the old, ineffective pattern of cursing God and my loved ones, and peppering myself with another round of negative self-talk.

In the heat of this round of negativity, I once again found myself transported back in time – to my sophomore year in high school. There I was, sitting all alone in my closet, sobbing uncontrollably. I had just lost my first home wrestling match of the year in a humiliating style. I was disgusted with myself and seriously considering calling my coach and quitting that very night. There was a knock on my closet door. My dad asked, "Jim, can I come in?" As I wiped tears of shame from my face and wondered if I was ready to face anyone, I whimpered, "Sure, Dad, come on in."

Dad sat on the floor without judging me and just checked in to see how I was doing. I spent a lot of time disclosing what was going on within me. After listening for a long time, he shared one of the most important lessons his own dad had ever taught him. He said, "Jim, your grandpa taught me that succeeding in life required each of us to learn how to turn minuses into plusses. Life always serves up a steady stream of tough challenges just like the one you're facing. If you can learn how to turn this minus into a plus, you'll be better suited to succeed later in life."

This time, I was mature enough to more deeply consider the wisdom that my dad was sharing. I decided to stay on the team and see if I could turn the minus of that humiliating evening into a plus that would prepare me for future success. Although I didn't know it then, my dad had bestowed another critical piece of a puzzle that would play a significant role in birthing the **Secret Seven-Word Question** that I'll reveal soon.

"This new voice was life-giving. It held the promise of tremendous possibility."

Back in the present, my high school memory gradually subsided as I noticed that the once powerful and disturbed source of my negative self-talk was once again losing its grip. It was gradually and unwillingly awakening an awareness of the powerful, noticing presence I mentioned earlier. This new voice was life-giving. It held the promise of tremendous possibility. It constantly encouraged the practice of self-reflection. Over and over, like the unbroken beat of a drum, it said, "Playfully, patiently persist in the practice of posing introspective questions and reflecting on them. Stronger questions will result in a stronger, more capable, more confident Jim."

As I continued to launder my mind of weak thoughts and negative self-talk, I noticed how the questions that surfaced seemed to be more refined and of ever-improving quality. They were more practical, and they held the promise of a richer reward.

Part Four

Divulging the Power of Introspective Questions

Practicality First, Profundity Later

I had a family to feed, so this new understanding demanded that I start posing some practical questions that could bring near-term benefit.

"How can I turn what I love to do into an abundant livelihood?"

As I ratcheted up the practicality of my questions, I began to take greater creative responsibility for my circumstances. I began to ask questions like these:

- What one thing can I do to improve my situation right now?

- What unique gifts and proven capabilities do I have to offer right now?

- What do I love to do?

- How can I turn what I love to do into an abundant livelihood?

- Who do I most want to serve?

These types of questions laid the foundation of my very first business, which I started back in the early 1990s. This business continues to thrive and provide valuable service, even in the midst of what the media is reporting to be one of the toughest economic times in decades.

What if What I Focus On Grows? Then What?

After many, many nights of pendulum-swinging between unpredictable outbursts of frustration and a fervid recommitment to my practice of posing and reflecting on meaningful questions, *something magical began to happen.* I began to notice that when I whined and complained, my life got worse. The more I moaned, the worse it got. Without limit!

On the other hand, when I posed uplifting and challenging questions and reflected on them, I noticed that:

- Creative ideas began to surface.
- Unexpected opportunities arose.
- Unanticipated resources appeared, seemingly out of nowhere.
- Caring, capable mentors and guides began to show up in my life.

Again, without limit!

A thought came to me.

What if what I focus on grows? Then what?

Once again, I've presented yet another potent seven-word question for your consideration. It's so mighty, in fact, that a group of very successful people combined creative forces to publish a book and produce a DVD focusing on their own version of this very question – *The Secret*. This project launched these folks' careers into another stratosphere of success. They've served millions of people worldwide and continue to make millions of dollars from this venture.

Now back to the point. Is this the **Secret Seven Word Question** that I've promised to reveal? The envelope please… rrrriiiipppp!

Well, although this question – *What if what I focus on grows?* – has been powerfully influential in my development, it is not the **Secret Seven Word Question** that I will unveil in a bit. I would, however, encourage you to invest some time reflecting on this one, for it too holds the powerful potential to dramatically improve the success, fulfillment, and happiness that you experience in life. Just let this seven-word beauty serve as a free, unexpected bonus!

As I continued to playfully inquire with self-reflective questions, I observed that I was becoming more aware. I started noticing more and more subtle dimensions of reality that had previously gone by undetected. As my subtler awareness deepened, the body of evidence mounted in support of the hypothetical idea that "what I focus on actually grows."

Through the awakening of this subtler awareness, I started to see the multiplicity of tools available to me that can help me consciously focus my attention and creatively influence my circumstances. These tools include my consciousness, intentions, beliefs, thoughts, feelings, words, and behaviors. As I gradually took

"This would require more than any other challenge I had undertaken."

creative responsibility for my life, it became apparent that to master this life, I'd have to develop the ability to:

- Consciously choose my intentions or goals.
- Feed and nurture them continuously.
- Carefully guide and orchestrate my thoughts, feelings, spoken words, behaviors, and self-talk to completely align themselves with my intentions or goals.

Although this idea excited me, it also humbled me. This would require more than any other challenge I had undertaken, including:

- Overcoming a speech impediment,
- Wrestling at the collegiate level,
- Reinvigorating my marriage,
- Raising a family, and
- Starting and sustaining a successful business.

I dug deep, hired a couple of coaches, and committed myself to do whatever life would require to successfully navigate the gauntlet of challenges ahead.

Practice Makes Perfect – The Emergence of Productivity Questions

If what I focus on grows, it would be essential to take creative control of what I was focusing <u>on</u>. As a result, I came to a new realization of just how important it was to have clearly stated priorities, goals, measures of success, and methods for celebrating success and holding myself accountable to capture key insights and apply them forward.

Over the years, I've attempted to implement many priority-

and goal-setting systems with some moderate success, but I never sustained my efforts. When I began to persistently apply this practice of posing questions in the context of clarifying my priorities and goals, momentum grew. Out of this momentum emerged a new breed of questions that honed my focus and provided greater clarity than any of the questions I'd tried up to that point. Some of my favorites include:

- How do I choose to invest my time, energy, and money?
- What will I accomplish this day/this week/this month/this year?
- What measures of success will I use to monitor my progress?
- How often will I monitor my progress?
- How will I acknowledge and celebrate my successes?
- How will I appreciate those who supported my success?

Part Five

Unveiling the Secret Seven-Word Wonder

Deeper Questions + Reflections = Unfathomable Meaning and Purpose

For about a decade, I continued this self-development practice of posing introspective questions. Over time, I began to feel called to explore a deeper set of questions.

"What might happen if I posed questions about aspects of myself that I knew the least?"

My priorities, goals, and successes were demanding a more meaningful foundation to rest on. I also wanted to develop a context that would more effectively integrate all the various aspects of my life.

This led me on an exploration. I wanted to see what might show up if I applied this introspective questioning practice to plumb the depths of my spiritual being. What might happen if I began to I pose questions to those aspects of myself that I knew the least? What if I didn't like what I found out? How long might this take? Would I have the patience and persistence that would be required? Did I have the courage to face what I might encounter?

There was only one way to find out. It was time to take the

plunge. And plunge I did. Some of my favorite questions from this realm include:

- Who am I?
- What is my fundamental reason for existing? (Another great seven-worder!)
- What do I feel compelled to create?
- What values will guide the way I treat others and myself?
- What generates and sustains happiness?

The beauty of these questions is that they required me to engage in some prerequisite learning if I wanted to experience practical benefits from posing them. These questions insisted that I learn to quiet my mind and calm my emotional field so I could hear and discern my own authentic responses. Whenever I would pose these questions in a disturbed mental or emotional state, I would be confused. The consistent response was always some form of "I don't know."

Learning to suspend my mental chatter and emotional noise continues to demand more of me than I ever could have imagined. This has tested my patience, challenged my capacity to persist, and commanded a quality of playfulness that I didn't know I possessed.

As I was growing up, I was conditioned to think that all questions had right answers that should be readily accessible. Twenty years of posing these deeper questions has helped me put this conditioned idea about questions to rest. The questions of purpose, vision, and values continue to yield deeper, more profound, more meaningful insights. I now suspect that my answers to these questions will never stop evolving. And for that I am grateful.

The Secret Seven-Word Question That's Transforming My Life

It's been almost 30 years now since life compelled me to start playfully, patiently, and persistently practicing this art of asking and reflecting on various questions. Undeniably, this practice has been one of the most productive and fulfilling development investments I've made in myself. I can't think of any other single practice that I've dedicated so much time and energy to. It has so richly blessed my life that I constantly find myself increasing the rigor with which I practice this discipline every day. The more I practice it, the more alive I become!

A few years back, a friend asked me, "Jim, if you were to boil down your 30 years of self-development work into one most important concept or practice, what would it be?" Now, I knew that my answer would absolutely reflect this practice of posing introspective questions to myself. I was, however, a bit shocked by how powerfully clear I was about one specific question that has been most productive for me over all these years. Without pause, I shared a radical seven-word question that has transformed my life. Nearly three decades of rigorous self-development work was distilled down to this one simple **Secret Seven-Word Question**: "WHY IS THIS PERFECT FOR ME NOW?"

Protest if You Must, But Don't Make the Mistake of Walking Away

Now you may be saying, "What!? <u>This</u> is the **Secret Seven-Word Question** I've been waiting for? What a waste of my time! I don't even know what this question really means or how it could possibly have a transforming effect on my life. I feel duped!"

"Running away would have robbed me of a priceless treasure that continues to enrich my life."

Not to worry. I completely understand. When I was first introduced to this idea, I protested too. Fortunately, I didn't listen to my narrow-minded, shortsighted tendency that wanted to act out its objection by storming away in disgust.

If I had, I'd be living a miserable existence. Running away would have robbed me of a priceless treasure that continues to enrich my life every day. Rather than run, I decided to put this concept to the test and see if it could produce any real benefit in my life. *I strongly recommend that you do the same!*

For centuries, wise, accomplished people from all walks of life, all ages, and all parts of the world have been suggesting the wonderful power hidden in this question. Our most influential philosophers, spiritual teachers, visionaries, texts, and proverbs have all hinted at the transformative power that can be revealed when posing the question, "Why is this perfect for me now?" My parents, coaches, and even my kids have illuminated me with quotes and stories that carefully mask the secret ingredients of this amazing question. Some of my more contemporary favorites:

- There is a silver lining in every dark cloud. – My mom
- Turn minuses into plusses. – My grandpa and my dad
- If life sh*ts on you, make fertilizer. – My son Mark
- Celebrate your critics and naysayers. They make you stronger. – Matt Furey

- The brightest stars can only be appreciated when contrasted by darkness. – Peter Ragnar

- If life gives you lemons, make lemonade. – Unknown

- Every adversity, every failure, every heartache carries within it the seed of an equal or greater benefit. – Napoleon Hill

- This very moment is the perfect teacher, and – lucky for us – it's with us wherever we are. – Pema Chodron

- Within every disaster is contained the seed of grace. – Eckhart Tolle

- Gracefulness is realizing the perfection in each moment, no matter what circumstances or challenges we face. – Peter Ragnar

- Every a**hole you encounter is actually a divine gift-giver of awareness in disguise. – Jim M Anderson

Although these contemporary wisdom-keepers lend credence to the potential benefits that may be revealed as you begin posing the **Secret Seven-Word Question** in your life, nothing lends more credence than your own direct experience. And that reminds me of a very important point I want to emphasize…

Don't Believe a Word I Say – Only Trust Your Own Direct Experience

At this moment, I want to emphasize a very important point. I don't want you to believe a word I say about the power of the **Secret Seven-Word Question** I've revealed. I want you to join me in rigorously testing it for validity. Join me in trying to find one moment that is <u>not</u> perfect for you now. I've been searching for an imperfect moment in my own experience for years now, and I've not yet succeeded. As a result, I'm enjoying life more than ever. The more perfection I look for, the more I seem to find.

Are you willing to join me in this quest? Say yes, begin the practice, and watch your life start to radically improve.

This Seven-Word Wonder Is a World Champion Question!

Of all the power questions I ever posed to myself, this **Secret Seven-Word Question** – "Why is this perfect for me now?" – is the *World Champion Question!*

There are no others that even come close for me.

Now, world championships aren't achieved overnight. Champions develop themselves over time. They rise to the top of the heap through relentless repetition and rigorous practice. This question has risen to the top of the question game in my life only because I have been so persistent in applying it. I've playfully practiced posing this question to myself thousands of times over the past decade or so. It works its magic with effortless ease and grace almost always.

When I first started playing with this question, I had to remove myself from the situation that was disturbing me and apply the question in a quiet, reflective place. Initially, I resisted the question and argued with it, but I kept on practicing.

In my early practice, I would often find that simply posing the question would actually <u>intensify</u> my mental or emotional disturbance. Some part of me seemed to be addicted to the disturbance and had a vested interest in making sure that I never got an answer to the question. I would really try hard to find perfection in what was happening

"Finding perfection in every moment can be accomplished only through unrelenting practice."

to me. But many times I'd come up short, failing to find
<u>anything</u> perfect about the situation I had allowed to rattle my
mind.

Once you catch a glimpse of perfection in the face of any
disturbance, you'll find yourself forever transformed. If you
can find one glimpse of perfection in a disturbance, you may
be able to find two. Two glimpses may lead to three. Three
glimpses hold the potential promise of four. If you can find
four glimpses of perfection in the face of this disturbance,
why not five, and on and on, potentially without limit?
Gradually, one tiny step at a time, perfection begins to reveal
itself in the midst of every disturbance you encounter.

At that point, you have your first verifiable, experience-based
evidence that perfection indeed resided in the face of one of
your life's challenges. The key here is to <u>persist in the
practice</u>. Continue to examine every disturbance, every
disruption, and every challenge to see if it presents something
of value, something that benefits you.

Just like any other skill, mastering the art of finding perfection
in every moment can be accomplished only through
unrelenting practice. In the sport of wrestling, I found that

building competence in executing a particular move would require 5,000+ repetitions before it would begin to flow naturally. I would see improvement and benefit with each repetition, but achieving <u>excellence</u> required an ongoing commitment to my practice. I had to practice a new move a couple of thousand times before successfully executing it in a match situation. After another few thousand reps in both practice sessions and real match conditions, I'd begin to develop the capacity to execute the move with perfection each time an opponent created the opening for that particular move.

I want to emphasize an important point I raised earlier. When you first begin playing with this question, you may find that you'll have to practice applying it in the privacy of a quiet place after a disturbing experience occurs. It may feel clumsy at first. You may feel frustrated or irritated by the seemingly ridiculous idea that a misfortune or challenge could actually contain a silver lining or a hint of perfection. That's OK. It's natural to feel this way when first learning a challenging skill. This is why you practice in the quiet of a private place at first, so you can build

"Experiencing perfection in this moment is the treasure of all treasures."

your confidence and capability before attempting to apply this idea live, in the midst of a real-life disturbance or challenge. Just be sure to keep on practicing. Before you know it, you'll find yourself instantly grateful for the perfection that is revealing itself to you in the moment of your life's challenges, dilemmas, and disturbances. And transformed you will be!

Part Six

Success Stories

This Question Is Designed to Be a Living Meditation

This question has become the most powerful living meditation I've ever practiced. Every day, life extends an infinite supply of opportunities to apply this question. Life is relentless, miserable, and unforgiving when I refuse to pose this world-champion question in the face of a challenge or disturbance. And the inverse is true as well. When I muster the courage to pose this question directly into the face of life's dilemmas, challenges, and seeming misfortunes, everything transforms right before my eyes – literally! In these moments, I open myself to experience life's extraordinary peace, luminescent quality, and unspeakable beauty. Experiencing perfection in this moment is the treasure of all treasures. It is worth whatever is required to enter its sacred halls.

Now, it wasn't this way at first. I used to get myself so wrapped up in life's disturbances that I would actually allow myself to be completely consumed by them. I'd sit in the negativity, attempt to curse it, demand that it leave me alone, and even try to project it onto others. These behaviors simply kept me stuck in the mud of my mental negativity, fruitlessly spinning my wheels, and digging myself into a deeper hole.

Show Me Some Proof

Now that I've laid a framework for understanding the potential benefits of this **Secret Seven-Word Question**, it's time to provide some proof. It's time to disclose some real-life situations where I've personally applied this discipline, actually finding perfection in the face of my life's challenges and dilemmas. Let's do it!

How could kidney disease possibly be perfect for me? It's a disease, for God's sake!

When I was experiencing kidney failure in the early '90s, I was overwhelmed with pain, doubt, and an intense fear that I might die. I felt abandoned by God. I felt I was the helpless victim of a completely random disease. My coach, Peter Ragnar, challenged me by asking, "Why are you resisting your situation so much? And by the way, are your fear, bitterness, and victim-hood helping to heal your condition, or is it further contributing to the disease?"

"What do you mean 'resisting'?" I protested. But then I stopped in my tracks and said, "Point well taken." As I struggled to rise out of my victim mindset and take responsibility for my condition, Peter shared a profound lesson on gracefulness. He said, "Jim, *gracefulness is recognizing the perfection in each moment, no matter what circumstances or challenges we face."* This idea resonated with me at a deep level. I examined the way I had been feeding my kidney disease with an overabundance of dis-eased thoughts, emotions, and negative self-talk. I genuinely wanted to embrace the truth of my circumstance and learn to handle it with a greater degree of grace and ease.

From that day, I began to gradually, step-by-step, change the way I related with my kidney system. I began to search for how my kidney disease was perfect for me now. I took time to learn more about what the kidney system is and what it does. An appreciation for this amazing system and my body's miraculous capacity to heal itself welled up within me. This prompted me to invest more time and energy in self-care disciplines and to take better care of my kidney system.

In addition, I began to examine why I was experiencing kidney disease and what it was here to teach me. I started searching to see if this experience might carry a hidden meaning that could actually benefit my life in the long run.

Three years of rigorous self-care resulted in a healthy kidney system, even though my right kidney lost function. My kidney disease had proven itself to be perfect for me.

Through this experience, I became aware that I had been subconsciously overwhelming my body with fearful thoughts and feelings, going all the way back to my birth. In addition, I had been severely dehydrating my body as a means of cutting weight for wrestling. Both of these habits had devastating consequences on my kidneys. Thanks to this experience, I've become much better at acknowledging and releasing fear from my system, and I now hydrate my body with plenty of pure water each day. I am forever grateful to my kidney system and for this experience and for the way it awakened me.

> *"Something magical begins to happen when I witness another human continuously choosing to search for the perfection in every dark cloud that they encounter."*

Mining for More Silver Linings in My Life's Dark Clouds

I've been blessed with a very rich and rewarding life. I delight in every experience I've had. Over the years, I've encountered intense storm clouds that presented the ideal practice fields for developing and road-testing the **Secret Seven-Word Question**. Here's a brief summary of some challenges I faced and the perfection that came from them:

Challenge	Perfection Realized
• Overcame a childhood speech impediment…	…learned to honor and appreciate diversity and differences.
• Recovered completely from a childhood heart disease…	…learned to appreciate my health, reducing the tendency to take it for granted.
• Abused my body by severely dehydrating it twice a week during my wresting career and feeding it junk food for many years, resulting in the loss of my right kidney…	…made me aware that conscious life was my highest priority, accentuated the critical importance of hydration, and revealed the devastating effects of repressing fear.
• Lost focus and passion in my life, which took me to the brink of divorce…	… reframed my priorities, held myself accountable to live them, and learned what authentic love and friendship require of me.
• Put my family at considerable risk by leaving the safety of a secure job to start my own business…	…found out I am valuable, and capable of creating, selling, and delivering world-class services that adapt and thrive in any economic conditions.

Challenge	Perfection Realized
• Parented five kids more effectively by inviting each of them to pose this question in the face of their challenges…	… learned to integrate the spirit of play into my practice of applying the **Secret Seven-Word Question.**
• Improved the effectiveness of my executive coaching by relentlessly inviting my clients to pose this question in the face of their challenges…	…realized that there is no limit to the beneficial application of this **Secret Seven-Word Question.**

Awed by the Courage of My Coaching Clients

As the global economic challenges have intensified over the past couple of years, my executive coaching clients have found themselves facing unprecedented leadership challenges. Day after day, I visit with men and women who tell me how overwhelmed they feel with the daunting predicaments they find themselves in.

Based on the stories I've shared in the preceding chapters, you now have a good sense of how relentless I am in posing this question to myself on a daily basis. I can assure you that when I work with my coaching clients, I'm as disciplined and rigorous in posing the **Secret Seven-Word Question** with them as I am with myself. I have been so consistent with the discipline of inviting them to apply this question that many of my clients are actually able to predict how I will respond after they finish airing out, complaining, or describing a problem they've encountered. Some of them even interrupt my response by saying, "I know, I know – why is this perfect for me now?" And after enjoying a spirited round of laughter together, I always follow up with, "Now that's a great question!"

Although I've been awed by the myriad ways that posing this question has enriched my life, something magical happens inside me when I have the privilege of witnessing another human being courageously choosing to search for the perfection that resides amid the dark, threatening, overwhelming clouds of intense challenge they encounter. Witnessing this is one of my life's richest treasures.

A Few Success Stories
I've Been Privileged to Witness

Success Story 1 – Job Loss in the Worst Economic Climate

A client recently told me that his boss had concluded that he was not the right person for the job. As a result, my client would be leaving the company in the next few months. He'd have to find work somewhere else.

Initially, this man felt devastated. He had become one of the statistics dominating the nightly news. He had become one of the many Americans whose job had disappeared as a global economic meltdown continued to strengthen its grip on the planet – another casualty in the long string of jobs that seemed to be tumbling like dominoes all across the United States.

"He overcame the emotional protest, and began to examine this ominous cloud that had darkened his life."

His self-confidence was shaken. Doubt and fear were clamoring to overtake his mind. As I settled into his office for our bi-monthly coaching session, I could feel the angst in the air as he shared the news. When he finished, I said, "Congratulations!" Trust me – that isn't what he expected to hear. As he sat quietly considering what to do with my response, I compassionately leaned forward and asked the **Secret Seven-Word Question**, "Why is this perfect for you now?"

I was awed by the courage this man displayed as he overcame the emotional protest he wanted to unleash on me, and began to examine this ominous cloud that had darkened his life. Is it possible that this situation could be perfect for him right now? Is it possible that there might actually be a silver lining in this storm cloud – hidden silver just waiting to be acknowledged, mined, appreciated, and fully enjoyed?

We spent the next couple of hours examining his situation through this rather unusual lens. As we explored, an amazing thing began to happen. The angst that filled the room at the beginning of our time together lifted. The energy had shifted from a strange concoction of worthlessness, shame, dread, and fear to a powerful atmosphere of pure possibility. This wonderful man's self-confidence began to return, worry gave way to hope, scarcity gave way to potential opportunity, and fear was replaced with newfound courage.

Over the next three months, this man found three tremendous opportunities. He assessed all of them and selected the one that would best benefit his family and serve his career aspirations. He chose a position that provided him with a better job, working for a boss who has a style that complements his own, at a company that is a better fit for him. He now delights in all the ways that his former situation was perfect for him in that moment.

I'm proud to report that he has once again become a statistic – and not the negative stats being hyped in the news. No, he's a statistic of a whole new type. He is one of the brave, bold, select few who chose to face his reality head on, mining the silver lining that this cloud offered him. I applaud him, and I'm inspired by his example. People like this encourage me to relentlessly return to my own daily application of the **Secret Seven-Word Question** in my life.

Success Story 2 – Creating an Opportunity Where None Existed

A few years back, I was working with a very successful woman who was investing a great deal of reflective time in clarifying her purpose and creating a career vision for herself. As this work progressed, it became clear that the role she was currently performing quite well was not truly aligned with her newly emerging vision.

Although she had a clear picture of the next job she was interested in, no such job existed in her company. She was supporting a family of four at the time, and it was not a good time to go looking for another job. She also loved the company and wanted to continue working there if possible.

Tension built as she felt a mounting sense of impossibility pressing in on her. On one hand, she wanted to move into a job that aligned with her compelling vision. On the other hand, she wanted to stay with her existing company. As the pressure built, I asked her, "Why is this perfect for you now?"

> *"What seemed impossible just weeks earlier had transformed itself into a perfect opportunity."*

She gave this a lot of thought. At first it seemed inconvenient. It seemed a bit cruel, because she was now clear about the perfect job that would challenge her and provide opportunities to grow, but no such job existed.

We began to search for the silver lining in this inopportune cloud. Suddenly it dawned on her that perhaps she could work with the senior team of the company to create a new role. As she began to explore various ideas, one of the vice presidents took a real interest in her suggestions. They worked together to create a new role. Then they built a business case to support the proposal. Guess what happened next?

The senior team unanimously agreed that this was a good idea, so they promoted someone into the job that my client vacated and she began her first day in the newly created role of her dreams in the company she wanted to work with. What seemed impossible just weeks earlier had transformed itself into a perfect opportunity.

She has been thriving in that job for a few years now and is continuing to grow by leaps and bounds. She is also more meaningfully engaged in her work than ever. As a result, this has become a win-win for everyone. She wins, her family wins, and the company wins!

Her seeming impasse turned out to be another silver-lined cloud, and she mined it beautifully by choosing to create what she wanted, in the place she wanted, even though it didn't appear possible. I love witnessing the creativity that flows from a human being who embraces the perfection that resides in something that appears to be anything but perfect.

Success Story Three – The Evaporating Retirement Fund

The news has been filled with stories of businesses closing, jobs cut, hiring freezes initiated, and stock portfolio values plummeting. The media and many news-watchers have been lathering up a fear-fest. Rather than continuing to beat the drum of negativity, piling on stories of doom and gloom, I want to share an inspiring story of a courageous exception.

I've been working with a client who was planning to retire in early 2009. A few months earlier, as we were formalizing his post-retirement plan, things looked positive. But then, the U.S. economy started to show significant signs of stress and strain, and the stock market took a sudden tumble. As the market responded to all the negative doom-and-gloom news, individual citizens found themselves in various states of shock as they watched their lifelong savings accounts and retirement funds began to evaporate.

> *"I recalled how profoundly this question serves me every time I face challenges, huge and small."*

The man I was coaching experienced a significant hit to his retirement account. As I prepared for our next session, I wondered how he would respond to this unforeseen challenge. I thought for sure that he would decide not to retire for another five years or so, sacrificing his plan for the ostensible security of continued, lucrative employment.

Deep inside, I also knew that this situation called for me to invite my client to call on the seven-word wonder, to ask himself, "Why is this perfect for me now?" I was honestly unsure whether I'd have the guts to ask this question – which might appear brash and insensitive at such a challenging time.

Then I recalled how profoundly this question serves me every time I face challenges, huge and small. Then, I remembered that this guy was a 20-year career marine. This strengthened my resolve. I knew that my client would have the best chance to work through this significant challenge if I could find the courage to pose the amazing **Secret Seven-Word Question**. On some level, I knew he had the stomach for it.

At our next coaching session, my client detailed the hit he had taken in the market. I felt awful for him and his family. Then (as I always do) I leaned in, looked deeply into this man's eyes, and with as much empathy as I could garner, asked, "Why is this perfect for you now?"

Much to my surprise, he responded, "Jim, I thought you might ask that, so I've been giving it a great deal of thought." He then began to list all the reasons why this was perfect for him right now! Then we rolled up our sleeves and began working on his post-retirement implementation plan, which would proceed as originally scheduled.

He is now happily retired and actively engaged in the things he was most passionate about doing. All the elements of his plan have been successfully implemented except one, and that one is likely to fall into place sometime soon.

I am awed by the example this man has set for me. Once again, I marvel at the power hidden in the courageous act of posing this question in the face of adversity.

Part Seven

Will the Seven-Word Secret Work for Me?

Putting this Secret Seven-Word Question to Work for You

This information will provide real value only if you put it to use. Oh sure – reading this book offers enough information to conceptually understand the power of this magnificent question. But a conceptual understanding that doesn't continually prove itself in your direct experience is about as valuable as a billion-dollar mansion built on a foundation of sand in Hurricane Alley. The only way you'll know the value of what I'm suggesting is to rigorously test it for its validity by relentlessly repeating the practice until you consistently experience its benefits first-hand.

You wouldn't have read this far if you weren't ready to begin posing this question in the face of your own life challenges. You have the capability, courage, and wherewithal to do this.

Now, armed with this seven-word secret, it's time to go hunting for an opportunity to apply it. The next time you feel a disturbance of any sort, take a breath and ask yourself, "Why is this perfect for me now?" And then observe what happens. Listen, and if you hear nothing but a round of angry protests, pose it again… and again… and again – until it begins to work its magic in your life.

Seven Simple but Profound Tips for Putting the Secret Seven-Word Question to the Test

Here are some tips that will support you as you begin the path of mastering the art of wielding the **Secret Seven-Word Question** with grace and ease, turning every misfortune into a priceless treasure.

1. Write the **Secret Seven-Word Question** on a card and carry it with you wherever you go. Always have it available to refer to whenever a disturbance presents itself. Once you notice the disturbance, reach into your pocket, pull out the card, and read the question. It may help to read it aloud at first, if the situation allows for it.

2. If you have not already done so, go to **http://fittolead.com** and sign up to receive my daily e-mail tips. These messages will offer practical ideas that will enhance your life by constantly applying this question. You'll also gain instant access to the Samurai of Self-Development's latest and greatest self-improvement ideas and inspirations.

3. Take a moment each evening to reflect on your day. Think back to situations that may have stirred you up earlier. If you're still bothered in the least bit by some occurrence, it's not too late to apply the question and free yourself of the disturbance. Take out your card, read the question, and reflect on the situation until you can find one thing that is perfect about it. Then, focus on that intensely until you feel the discomfort in your chest lighten up and transform into a spirit of gratitude. Feel the appreciation building in your heart center. Find a creative way to express your appreciation for the perfection that this situation brought into your awareness.

4. Be playful in your practice. Bring a childlike spirit. If you take this too seriously, you'll miss tons of silver linings in the storm clouds you encounter. By lightening up a bit, you relax, and being in a relaxed state makes it much easier to find the perfection that always eludes you when you're disturbed.

5. Be persistent in your practice of posing this question to yourself. This practice will benefit you the very first time you apply it. But these benefits will increase and

magnify the more you consistently hold yourself accountable to doing it, day in and day out. Just like anything else, relentless repetition will forge greatness over time.

6. Be patient in your practice. The most meaningful and fulfilling things in life take time. Whenever you feel like giving up, read your card and apply the question. The disturbance that is trying to get you to give up will evaporate, and your commitment to this practice will once again victoriously reassert itself.

7. Finally, DO NOT, I repeat, DO NOT pose this question to your family members, co-workers, and friends when you see them stewing in a disturbed state of mind. It takes years of practice to master the art of posing this question to yourself before you'll be prepared to effectively invite others to do the same. Save yourself a lot of grief and just trust me on this one. It's not by chance that I referred to this as the **Secret Seven-Word Question** throughout this book. It's intended to be a secret that you keep to yourself, that you apply only to yourself.

Summary of My Seven Simple but Profound Tips:

1) Write it on a card.

2) Get inspiration.

3) Reflect daily.

4) Be patient.

5) Be persistent.

6) Be playful.

7) Keep it to yourself.

I wish you the very best as you put this secret to work in your life. I'd love to hear your success stories as you begin to find silver linings in the dark clouds you encounter. Send your success stories to the Samurai of Self-Development at samurai@fittolead.com.

Appreciative Epilogue

An Expression of Special Thanks To Some Exceptional People

I am grateful to my family, friends, and coaches for all the ways they have encouraged, supported, and challenged me throughout my life. Each and every human being I encounter enriches my life beyond measure.

I would like to express special gratitude to:

- **My soulmate and best friend Kristan** for her infinite love, priceless friendship, willingness to walk the spiritual path with me, and especially for her capacity to consistently discern and speak the truth. The magic I experience in our connection cannot be expressed in words.

- **My children and teachers Ben, Jonathon, Sarah, Mark, and Susan** for the good fortune you have attracted into my life. Thank you for the love, joy, wisdom, laughter, and support you have provided me during my darkest days. Your births are among my most perfect moments, and your lives are among my most precious blessings.

- **My Mom and Dad,** who planted the seed for this book in my heart at an early age. Thank you, Mom and Dad, for bringing me into the world and for providing me with such an amazing example of how to live life to its fullest and to rigorously search for silver linings in every dark cloud.

- **My friend and editor, Veronica**, whose love for words, annual gifts of poetry, and enthusiasm for exploring conscious life have formed the foundation of an extraordinary friendship. Witnessing your journey from master editor into a full-fledged author has inspired me to pick up my pen and see what all the fuss is about. I now share your love of the written word and plan to continue writing for years to come. Thank you also for extending your incredible talents and gifts in support of this book.

- **My family members Chris, Dan, Martha, Jenny, Tim, Denton, Carol, Tovie, Ty, Todd, Amy, Christy, Kevin, Mac, Mark, and Steve,** who have willingly walked alongside me in both the best and worst of times. Your friendship, wise counsel, passion for the written word, and loving encouragement have blessed me beyond measure.

- **A sacred circle of friends and wisdom keepers who are called Tracy, Maggie, Meg, Barbara, Roger, Chick, Jerry, Bob, Dan, David, Barbara, Tony, and Jerry** who have invited me to join them in plumbing the depths of human consciousness, sharing the commensurate tears, surrender, joy, laughter, and illumination that continue to present themselves along the way. Thank you for being there to laugh, love, challenge, stretch, and inspire me to persist in my writing and to open myself to fuller conscious creative expression.

- **Each coaching client I have had the privilege to serve,** Thank you for inviting me to join you in supporting your intention to transform your effectiveness as human beings and as leaders. I am deeply appreciative that you invited me to join you in co-exploring the wild frontier of consciousness expansion. Your courageous commitment to personal transformation inspires me beyond words.

- **Two superlative coaches named Peter Ragnar and Matt Furey.** When I was facing my greatest challenges, I asked myself this question: "What world-class coaches are best equipped to guide me in my climb up the mountain of human excellence?" Over a two-decade period, I have been blessed with the guidance and counsel of two of the finest human beings I've ever had the privilege to meet – **Peter Ragnar** (**www.roaringlionpublishing.com**) and Matt Furey (**www.mattfurey.com** and **www.psycho-cyb.com**).

Peter has been coaching me for almost two decades. His collection of products, books, courses, seminars, and individual coaching programs have been life-changing for me. He has done an extraordinary job supporting my intentions to:

- Examine and implode my dysfunctional beliefs,
- Hone my rational mind,
- Notice cause-and-effect relationships,
- Trust my intuition,

- Test each and every belief I have for its validity,
- Awaken my noticing presence,
- Reclaim creative responsibility for my life, and
- Recognize conscious life as my highest priority.

Peter leads by example and boldly dares to go where most mortals would consider impossible. He is a pre-Baby Boomer who is a successful entrepreneur, bestselling author, accomplished artist and musician, Black Belt instructor of Shingitai Jujitsu who continues to perform world-class feats of strength on a regular basis, and he's healthier than most 20-year-olds I know. He accomplishes all of this while enjoying a secluded, peaceful lifestyle with the love of his life, Ann. They live in a true state of abundance where they experience more than enough time, energy, and money to do whatever pleases them.

I met Matt Furey in 2001. His quiet, powerful presence commanded my immediate attention and respect. I bought his bestselling book, **Combat Conditioning,** the very next day. His perspective on functional fitness and his world-class body weight exercises have forever changed the way I train.

In 2003, I attended my first Matt Furey seminar. As always, Matt over-promised and then over-delivered. I invested $1,500 and walked away with at least $15,000 of value.

Shortly after that, I began my first Matt Furey coaching program and have continued to invest in his coaching every year since 2005. He has done an extraordinary job supporting me in learning to:

- Value myself;
- Magnetize, appreciate, and enjoy money;
- Celebrate critics and naysayers;
- Turn a struggling business into a collection of valuable companies;
- Obliterate my fear of selling;
- Unplug my automatic failure mechanism and tune up my automatic success mechanism;
- Open myself to the possibility of Zero Resistance Living®;
- Succeed with his "Theatre of the Mind" discipline; and
- Deepen my appreciation for the art of posing questions.

Matt also practices what he preaches. He never stops stretching, improving, innovating, building, and succeeding. He proves how much he cares about his coaching clients by the degree to which he consistently gives of himself to support our success. He continues to over-promise and significantly over-deliver on those lofty promises. Matt is a successful entrepreneur, self-made multimillionaire, world-class self-development coach, Internet marketing genius, bestselling author, fitness and self-defense expert, NCAA champion wrestler, and world champion martial artist. He is also a dedicated husband and father.

For more information on other products, membership programs, and coaching groups offered by Fit To Lead, contact us:

On the web at:

www.fittolead.com

Via e-mail at:

jim@fittolead.com

or

Via direct mail at:

Fit To Lead
768 Stagecoach Blvd.
Evergreen, CO 80439

About the Author

Jim M Anderson is a successful entrepreneur, world-class executive coach, and author. He was born and raised in Northwest, Ohio. Jim attended The Ohio State University where he majored in Economics and served as captain of the wrestling team. After graduating, Jim married his best friend, Kristan. They were blessed with the stewardship of five amazing children who are now thriving on their own. Jim spent the first 15 years of his career leading and engaging teams in navigating tremendous change in a corporate family business setting. Then in 1992, he ventured out to start his first business, Key-Connections Inc., a strategic consulting and executive coaching firm headquartered in Evergreen, CO. Over the past 18 years, Jim has served clients in organizations such as Boeing, Molson-Coors, Exempla Healthcare, Textron, University of Notre Dame, The Leadership Circle, Hamilton Farm Bureau, and Federated Media. He is also a founder of Fit To Lead, a new web-based information publishing company dedicated to creating and distributing top-notch leadership development tools. Jim loves serving individuals and organizations interested in improving their effectiveness and developing a deeper sense of market-tested self-awareness.

Made in the USA
San Bernardino, CA
18 August 2016